• • THE LIBRARY OF FAMOUS WOMEN • •

BENAZIR
BHUTTO

Prime Minister

by
Elizabeth Bouchard

A BLACKBIRCH PRESS™ BOOK

THE ROSEN PUBLISHING GROUP, INC.

Published by Blackbirch Press™ in conjunction with The Rosen
Publishing Group, Inc., 29 East 21st Street, New York, NY 10010

©1992 Blackbirch Press™ a division of Blackbirch Graphics, Inc.
First Edition

Printed in Hong Kong
Bound in the United States of America

Editors: Kailyard Associates
Art Director: Cynthia Minichino

Library of Congress Cataloging-in-Publication Data

Bouchard, Elizabeth.
    Benazir Bhutto: prime minister / Elizabeth Bouchard.
    (The Library of famous women)
    "A Blackbirch Press book."
    Includes bibliographical references and index.
    Summary: Examines the life of Pakistan's first woman prime
minister against the background of the politics of her country.
    ISBN 0-8239-1205-1
    1. Bhutto, Benazir—Juvenile literature. 2. Prime ministers—
Pakistan—Biography—Juvenile literature. [1. Bhutto, Benazir. 2. Prime
ministers. 3. Pakistan—Politics and government.] I. Title. II. Series.
DS389.22.B48868 1991
954.9105'092—dc20
[B]   91-29290
                                                   CIP
                                                   AP

Contents

Chapter 1

The Oldest Child of an Old Family

On June 21, 1953, in the blistering heat of a Pakistan summer, Benazir Bhutto was born. Benazir's parents, Nusrat and Ali Bhutto, nicknamed their first child Pinkie because her skin was so rosy. Outside their quiet hospital room, the city of Karachi baked on the shores of the Arabian Sea. To the east lay the great Indus River. The fertile banks of this river hold the richest farmlands in the country. It is here, in the province called Sind, that thousands of people and dozens of villages bear the name of Benazir's family: Bhutto.

Benazir in 1972, at age 18.

The Bhutto Family

Much of the farmland in Sind belonged to the Bhutto tribe. For several centuries, Benazir's family had the largest land holdings in Sind. Since her great-grandfather's time, Benazir's family has lived near the

(Opposite page)
A street scene in Larkana, the area in which Benazir's family has lived for generations.

5

town of Larkana. Their lands were measured in miles, not acres. But even their riches and power did not protect them completely from the Western conquerors, the British.

Benazir's great-grandfather, Murtaza Bhutto, enraged the British by eloping with a British woman. He paid for this crime dearly. Murtaza had to flee the country, and the British took all of his lands. The family home was auctioned. Their silk carpets and satin sofas were sold. So were their silver and gold plates. They auctioned off the huge cooking pots that cooked for thousands on holidays, and the embroidered tents that guests sat under.

Eventually a deal was worked out. Murtaza returned to Larkana, but only to die from poisoning at the age of 27. His son, Benazir's grandfather, was made a knight—Sir Shah Nawaz Bhutto—for his services to the British.

At the beginning of this century Benazir's grandfather, Sir Shah Nawaz, was considered very progressive because he educated the women in his family. In the matter of marriage, however, he was traditional. In Sind at this time, all wealth lay in property. Islamic law (the laws of the Muslim religion) allowed women to inherit

❋

"Benazir's grandfather . . . was considered very progressive because he educated the women in his family."

A statue of Queen Victoria stares down at a group of Pakistanis in Karachi, Pakistan's capital. The area was ruled by the British until 1947, when Pakistan declared its independence.

property. Therefore, the only way to keep land in the family was to arrange a marriage within the family, between first or second cousins.

When he was only 12, Benazir's father, Ali, was married to his cousin, Amir. She was eight or nine years old at the time. When she was old enough to leave home, she moved to the Bhutto family home. Amir stayed there for the rest of her life and was known as "Number One Wife."

Ali was sent to the United States to study, to see firsthand the advances being made in the West. He studied hard and graduated with honors. After that he studied law

The Bhutto family sits together for a photograph in 1979. From left are Nusrat, Shah Nawaz, Ali, and Benazir. In front are Mir and Sanam (Sunny).

at Oxford University in England. Then he returned to Pakistan to practice law.

Benazir's mother, Nusrat, was the daughter of a wealthy Iranian businessman. She grew up in the city of Karachi in a modern style. In the countryside, the Bhutto women lived in *purdah*, behind walls and under veils. In contrast, Nusrat and her sisters did not wear veils. They even drove their own cars. This was forbidden to most

Muslim women. Most importantly, Nusrat had a college education.

It is easy to see how Nusrat seemed like the perfect wife to the young, Western-educated Ali Bhutto. The Muslim religion allows a man to have up to four wives, and it was in the Bhutto family tradition for men to marry more than once. Nusrat and Ali were married in 1951. Nusrat became "Number Two Wife."

Benazir was the first child of Ali and Nusrat. In most families, the first child has a special position, and this was true of the Bhuttos, too. In Pakistan's culture, boys were usually favored over girls. But that was not true in the Bhutto family. As the oldest, Benazir was spoiled by all sides of the family.

Soon the Bhutto children numbered four. A brother, Mir, was born a year after Benazir. Then came her sister, Sanam (Sunny for short), and finally the baby of the family, a boy named Shah Nawaz. All four Bhutto children lived happily as the sons and daughters of one of Pakistan's richest families. At the time, no one yet knew that all of these children would eventually spend years forbidden to live in their native country.

*

The Muslim religion allows a man to have up to four wives.

Chapter 2

Growing Up in Karachi

Ali Bhutto could not be the lawyer and politician he wanted to be on the rural estates of Larkana. This young man had studied at the best universities in the West. He wanted to be a leader and to modernize his country.

Benazir, on the day she was elected president of the Oxford Union. She was only the third woman to hold that office.

Pakistan was a young country. In 1947, this mainly Muslim part of India had separated from the mainly Hindu part. Both India and the newly created Pakistan had just become independent from Great Britain. Now was the time to develop a modern, powerful nation out of a poor and backward colony.

Ali Bhutto's father had built a fine, large house for the family on the outskirts of Karachi. It was modern in the sense that there were no separate quarters for the women of the family.

Benazir grew up in a kind of luxury hardly known here. The house was roomy enough to sleep many of the Bhutto clan.

(Opposite page)
Benazir wears Pakistan's traditional *shalwar khameez* for a formal portrait.

On holidays this could number in the twenties. The floors and walls were hung with valuable old carpets. The sitting rooms contained many fine English antiques. The grounds around the house were spacious. They bloomed with coconut palms, mangoes, and red and yellow flowering trees from the Karachi desert. In the broiling summer heat, the family was cooled by breezes from the Arabian Sea.

Families kept house in much the same way as they had for centuries. Labor was very cheap, and it was the custom for well-to-do people to keep servants. The Bhuttos had a staff of about 21. The servants took care of all the daily household tasks: cleaning, laundry, going to the market, cooking, making repairs, screening callers, gardening, and looking after the personal needs of the Bhuttos.

Study Hard

Luxury did not mean that the Bhutto children could just play all day. Education had top priority in the Bhutto household. Ali Bhutto planned to change the status of women in Pakistan. And he wanted to make his own family an example. Benazir began to attend nursery school at the age of three. At five, she entered a convent school run by Irish nuns. It was supposed to be the best school in Karachi for preparing students to live in an international world. All the lessons were in English. By the time Benazir graduated at age 16, she had studied for over 10 years in English.

Of course, Benazir would learn many languages. All educated Pakistanis could speak English. They also knew Urdu, the national language of Pakistan. The native language of Benazir's father was Sindi. That was the language spoken in the province where she grew up. Benazir's mother was from the neighboring country of Iran. She spoke Persian in her family. At home, however, Benazir and her parents spoke mostly English.

Multi-language families like Benazir's are not unusual. In Pakistan, there are 24 official languages. Some are written in the Roman alphabet, like English. Others are written in Arabic script. Still others are written in Sanskrit, the ancient language of the Indian sub-continent. In order to communicate with one another, Pakistanis try to learn at least one or two common tongues; especially English.

Students are required to learn English in most countries of the world. But this is not because English is a superior language.

Cars and buses share the downtown avenues with buffalo in Pakistan's old capital of Rawalpindi.

Pakistani women show the identity cards they need to vote. Traditionally, women were not given these cards, and were prevented from participating in their government.

Rather, English is the language of modernity. It contains the words needed to talk about computers, nuclear physics, medicine, and other sciences. English is the language of business, technology, diplomacy, and tourism.

Ali Bhutto told his children that they must do well in their studies. Even when he was traveling, he paid close attention to their grade reports. When they were older, he hired tutors to instruct them in English and math. Every afternoon after school, Benazir would spend several hours doing homework and extra reading.

Although this was surely enough education for any little child, Benazir had one more subject: religion. Like most Pakistani families, the Bhuttos were Muslim. The children had to learn to read their bible, the Holy Koran, in its original language, Arabic. So after her school studies, Benazir would spend an hour every day struggling with Arabic. She memorized lessons and instructions on how to behave. Many of the lessons are like those Christians learn in Sunday School.

Benazir's mother taught her the rituals of Islamic prayer. When Benazir was nine years old, Nusrat would come into her room at dawn for morning prayer. Out-

side, the *muezzin* called the faithful to
prayer from the tower of Karachi. Inside,
Benazir and Nusrat would wash their
hands, feet, and faces so that they would be
pure before God. Then they would lie
down on the floor facing west toward
Mecca, the holy city, and say prayers. This
was to be done five times every day.

Doing well in school was not Benazir's
only responsibility. When she was four
years old and her father 28, Ali was sent to
represent Pakistan at the United Nations in
New York. This and many other government posts meant that he was away from
home much of the time. Nusrat traveled
with him, and the four children remained
at home with the household staff.

As the oldest, Benazir was expected to
look after the smaller children. In a family
with many servants, this did not mean
feeding the youngest ones or changing
diapers. It meant thinking about the wel-
fare of the others, a habit that would influence Benazir's life much later.

Being a Girl

In a more traditional family, growing up
might have meant imprisonment for
Benazir. Not actually in a public prison,
but in a private one of *purdah*. In Pakistan,

and particularly in Sind Province, once women married they were seldom allowed to leave the four walls of their house. One night, she overheard her mother and father talking. Nusrat was asking her husband if he planned to continue the tradition of marrying his children to cousins to keep the land in the family. Benazir must have held her breath for her father's answer.

"I don't want the boys to marry their cousins and leave them behind our compound walls. And I don't want my daughters buried alive behind some other relative's compound walls," he said. "Let them finish their educations first. Then they can decide what to do with their lives."

One day, Benazir and her mother were traveling by train from Karachi to Larkana. Nusrat pulled out a black, gauzy cloth, just like the one she was wearing.

"You are no longer a child," she said. She draped the *burqa* over her daughter. The black veil covered her dress and arms. It was hot and made movement difficult. And, the narrow eye-slits took the color out of the world and turned it gray.

When they arrived home, Nusrat mentioned to Ali that Benazir had worn her *burqa* for the first time. Benazir remembers there was a long pause.

✳

"She doesn't need to wear it," her father said finally. ". . . The best veil is the veil behind the eyes. Let her be judged by her character and her mind, not by her clothing."

"She doesn't need to wear it," her father said finally. "The Prophet Muhammed himself said that the best veil is the veil behind the eyes. Let her be judged by her character and her mind, not by her clothing." This decision was to cause Ali Bhutto a lot of trouble later on.

Benazir was happy. "I became the first Bhutto woman to be released from a life spent in perpetual twilight," she wrote. From then on, in public, Benazir would wear the *shalwar khameez,* the baggy pantaloons and tunic that are the national dress of men and women in Pakistan.

In 1972, Benazir stood next to her father, then president of Pakistan, Ali Bhutto. Bhutto had completed talks with India's Prime Minister Indira Ghandi, center. India's Foreign Minister, Swaran Singh is second from right.

17

Chapter 3

An Education
for Democracy

Benazir arrived with her mother at Harvard Yard in Cambridge, Massachusetts, in the fall of 1969. At 16, she was younger than most of her classmates. Having never spent an hour away from her family and small circle of girlfriends, she was also very shy. How would she get along with so many strangers? Would she be able to compete at such a university?

Nusrat stayed for the first two weeks to help Benazir settle. She had brought a fine woolen *shalwar khameez* for her daughter, to keep her warm in the icy New England winters. Nusrat also spent time calculating the direction of Mecca so Benazir would know in which direction to pray.

The *shalwar khameez* soon disappeared into a closet. It was much too exotic for classes, and it made Benazir stand out among the rest of the students. Soon she

Benazir, as she appeared in the early 1970s.

(Opposite page)
Ali Bhutto, as foreign minister of Pakistan, addresses the United Nations in September of 1965.

Civil war between East Pakistan and West Pakistan took a great toll in lives.

was in jeans and a sweatshirt, eating peppermint ice-cream and attending rock concerts. She grew her hair long in the style of Joan Baez, the folk singer. These were the days of the student movement against the Vietnam War. Campuses around the country rocked with protests. "U.S. Out of Vietnam!" shouted the protesters. Benazir was among them.

Feminism was another campus issue. If anyone knew about the unequal position of women, it was the young woman from Pakistan. She had been lucky. She had escaped the dreaded black veils and high walls of *purdah*. But most women at home were uneducated and invisible. Now she was able to imagine what true equality could be like. She stayed up at night talking with her friends about their hopes for careers and a new kind of relationship with men. In her own family she had not been forced to see marriage as her main goal, but that was unusual. At Radcliffe, everyone was thinking about the war, and it was liberating.

Crisis in Pakistan gave a sharp edge to her studies in government. An independent movement was growing in East Pakistan, which was separated by 1,000 miles from the Western part. As the country moved toward civil war, Benazir's father was made foreign minister. Benazir says he opposed the use of force and was sickened when the Pakistani Army attacked the East's capital city of Dacca.

. . . Most women at home were uneducated and invisible. Now she was able to imagine what true equality could be like.

For Benazir, it was agony to read of the looting, raping, killing, and burning that the American press was reporting. She couldn't believe it. She found herself in heated arguments with classmates, defending Pakistan against charges of cruelty. Then India invaded Pakistan.

A week after the invasion, her father arrived in New York to attend a U.N. Security Council session. Benazir went to meet him. She sat behind him in the council room as the United States, China, the Soviet Union, India, and other members debated whether or not to intervene. Ali Bhutto made several fiery speeches calling for a cease-fire, the withdrawal of Indian forces, and the stationing of U.N. peacekeeping forces in the area.

Each superpower, of course, was most concerned with protecting its own interests. Ali Bhutto's role was to convince each of these powerful countries that supporting Pakistan was in its interest. One way to do that was to play on the fears they had of each other.

In her father's hotel suite, the Soviet delegation came and went. So did George Bush, who was heading the U.S. delegation. Benazir helped to take calls.

In spite of his efforts, a bad end came quickly. Ali Bhutto realized that the superpowers were supporting India. He and his delegation walked out and returned to Pakistan. A few days later, 6,000 miles away, Benazir watched on television as the general of Pakistan's defeated army surrendered his sword to the Indian commander. With the help of India, East Pakistan had been separated from West.

The people were furious. The capital city was in flames, the president was forced to resign. Ali Bhutto had been made foreign minister and deputy prime minister during the war. Now he became president.

President Bhutto's Daughter

In 1973, Benazir graduated with honors from Radcliffe. She wanted to join her country's diplomatic corps. But she hoped first to spend a year in graduate school. Her father said no. It would be better for her not to stay in one place too long, he argued. He said that because she was Pakistani, she must not set roots in the United States, and must have other experiences.

Ali Bhutto rides through his native town of Larkana after his release from a two-month prison term in 1968.

Reluctantly, Benazir went to England to study at Oxford University. Her father had studied there, and many foreign leaders had also attended this important international center. While her father began the painful task of rebuilding his war-torn country, Benazir studied international affairs at Oxford.

Oxford was not as relaxed and friendly as Radcliffe had been. But Benazir now knew how to make friends. At her father's urging, she joined the debate team. Here, students held formal debates on issues of great international importance. What better training for a budding diplomat!

By the time she became president of Oxford's most famous political club, Benazir had become a confident public speaker. Here, she addresses the 1989 Harvard graduating class.

Benazir had begun to erase all traces of her childhood shyness at Radcliffe. Now she became a confident public speaker. In January 1977, nearly three years after she entered Oxford, Benazir became president of this famous political club. Then she and her brother Mir, who was a freshman at Oxford, flew home to Pakistan for spring break.

Real-World Politics

Ali Bhutto and his PPP party, the Pakistan Peoples Party, had just won a stunning

election victory when his children arrived
home. Yet, things seemed to be falling
apart. Bhutto had once warned foreigners
that countries like Pakistan were fragile
and hard to rule. And, indeed, Bhutto was
having trouble holding power. One enemy
was the military, which resented giving
power to civilians. The rich landowners
were angry because some of their huge
farmlands had been given to poor farmers.
The rich factory owners opposed Bhutto
because some of their plants had been
taken over by the government. And the
tribal rulers in the Western provinces resented any attempts to weaken their power.
All this made for a dangerous situation.
The opposition used strikes, rallies, and
walkouts to threaten the government. Ali
Bhutto struck back with arrests. To com-
plicate matters, the United States was less
and less friendly toward Bhutto. They did
not like his policies of land reform and
nationalizing industry. They also feared
that Pakistan was trying to build a nuclear
bomb. No help for Bhutto would come
from the United States. And many Pakistanis believed the CIA was plotting against
him. Only a month after Benazir returned
home, the situation turned critical.

Chapter 4

Imprisonment

In the early morning hours of July 5, 1977, the Pakistan army seized power in a military *coup* (takeover). The man who ordered the coup was the chief of the army, General Zia. He was a quiet man and a strict Muslim. Ironically, he had been appointed by Ali Bhutto, who felt he could trust him.

The highest government officials were rounded up first. Benazir recalls that her father found out about the coup from a policeman who had seen the army surrounding the prime minister's home.

Soon, the entire family was awake and huddled around the telephone as Ali put in a call for General Zia. The general had just been at the Bhutto house the day before. Then he had assured the president of the army's loyalty. But now Zia himself came to the telephone and explained his reasons for the coup. The opposition

Benazir in the early 1980s.

(Opposite page)
After her release from prison in 1986, Benazir continued to speak out against General Zia. Here, Benazir sits below a painting of her father, who was executed by order of Zia.

parties had complained that Bhutto's party had rigged the elections. Zia said he needed to hold Ali Bhutto in "protective custody" for 90 days. He promised to hold new elections afterwards. He was sure that Ali Bhutto would then be re-elected.

Benazir's brother Mir wanted to resist the military. "Never resist a military coup," Ali answered quietly. "The generals want us dead. We must give them no pretext to justify our murders." Together, the family waited for the officers to come and take Ali Bhutto away.

For some time, Ali Bhutto was held at a government rest home in Larkana. Then, curiously, he was released, but only briefly. The Bhutto's guessed that Zia thought Ali and his family would flee the country. Or that he would lose his popularity with the Pakistani people. Neither happened. Ali and his family met with PPP leaders and supporters. Crowds gathered wherever they went. It became clear that Bhutto was still a leader in Pakistani politics. Then, one night, soldiers invaded his home and took him to jail. He was charged with planning to murder a political opponent, a crime that held the death penalty.

Zia's first act after the coup was to suspend the constitution, the first Pakistan

❋
"The generals want us dead. We must give them no pretext to justify our murders."

ever had. In doing that, he wiped away all laws and all rights of the people. Then he cancelled the elections he had promised, and outlawed political parties. Realizing the danger to his family, Ali Bhutto told Mir, Shah, and Sunny to return to their colleges abroad. They would need their education, he told them. Nusrat took over the leadership of the outlawed PPP, and Benazir stayed to help her. Soon they were both arrested.

The Death of Ali Bhutto

In the early morning hours of April 4, 1979, 28-year-old Benazir and her mother lay awake, staring into the dark. They were locked up in a deserted police training camp. A few miles away, in a primitive jail cell, was Ali Bhutto, Benazir's father.

He lay on a mattress on the floor, near a stinking hole that led to the sewer. He was thin and sick from two years of mistreatment. For the last 10 days he had refused food. His trial, which had dragged on for months, was rigged. The government's witnesses contradicted themselves and each other. At times, Zia's hand-picked judge put words in their mouths. When the court finally sentenced Ali Bhutto to death, the world was horrified. Around

General Muhammed Zia al-Haq seized control of the Pakistani government in July, 1977, over-throwing Ali Bhutto.

❋

. . . It stank of mildew and rot. At about two o'clock in the morning, Benazir began shaking with cold, despite the heat.

the globe, the leaders of many countries appealed to General Zia to pardon Bhutto.

Benazir remembers the night when she and her mother lay in the heat of their cell. The cell was made up of several small rooms with cracked cement floors, and it stank of mildew and rot. At about two o'clock in the morning, Benazir began shaking with cold, despite the heat. She and her mother huddled together the rest of the night. By dawn, she knew her father was dead. He had been executed by order of General Zia, the military dictator of Pakistan.

Years of Imprisonment

For the next seven years, Benazir was in and out of jail. Some of the time, she was under house arrest, either in Larkana or in Karachi. In some ways, house arrest was better than being in jail. Home was cool and clean. She could shower and read, but she was seldom allowed to have visitors, and she was never allowed to leave. Sometimes the telephone worked, more often it didn't.

All of the changes that her father had brought about had been quickly erased. In the factories and on the farms, union leaders were being arrested and the union contracts torn up. Many people who had supported Ali Bhutto lost their jobs and homes and had to flee the country.

Suddenly, like their neighbor Iran, Pakistan was becoming an Islamic state. Non-Muslims, who under Ali Bhutto had all the rights of a citizen, were discriminated against. Public executions and beatings were authorized and carried out. The cutting off of a hand and the stoning of women to death for adultery became legal punishments.

Whenever they were released from confinement, Benazir and her mother spoke out against the government's cruelty. Soon they would be back under arrest. Their lives had never been in such danger as in March 1981, when a Pakistani airliner was hijacked. The hijackers belonged to a terrorist group. They demanded freedom for some 20 political prisoners held in Zia's jails. The plane was sent to a neighboring country, where Mir and Shah were living in exile. Benazir's brothers met the hijackers at the airport and embraced them as the press looked on.

The hijacking turned out to be a blessing for Zia. The PPP and other parties had just united their efforts to end the military rule. For the first time, they could really

Benazir addresses supporters at her home in 1986. She had just been released after a month-long arrest for ignoring a government ban on public rallies.

Benazir's mother, Nusrat Bhutto, spent many years working with her daughter to organize the PPP.

challenge Zia's power. Now, however, Zia had an excuse to use drastic measures against the opposition, especially the Bhutto women. Zia wanted to implicate them in terrorist activity, to be rid of them once and for all. Thousands of activists were arrested and tortured in an attempt to get "confessions." Benazir and her mother were arrested once again. For Benazir, that meant solitary confinement in a freezing jail.

She was certain she would die. Her jailers brought her new rumors daily. One rumor said she was to be taken to a torture center and forced to confess her involvement in the hijacking.

The jail conditions were terrible. Both Benazir and her mother had to be hospitalized during their confinement. By summer, the heat was fierce. Windstorms from the desert blew through the cell and turned it into a sticky oven. Benazir's skin split and peeled, coming off her hands in sheets. Boils erupted on her face, and her hair fell out in handfuls. Grasshoppers, mosquitos, stinging flies, bees, and cockroaches invaded the cell, biting and stinging her day and night.

The filth, heat, and stress of imprisonment took its toll on her health. A doctor who treated her for an ear infection pierced her eardrum, causing painful infections. Had he done it on purpose? Benazir didn't know, but she became terrified of the doctors. If Zia could kill her father after a fake public trial, surely he could find a doctor or hospital who would do the same thing quietly.

Zia did release the 20 political prisoners to the hijackers, but he arrested thousands of new ones. Nusrat, Benazir's mother, was eventually diagnosed as having lung cancer. She was allowed to leave the country for medical treatment in the West. Meanwhile, Benazir was let out of jail and put under house arrest.

Help came from an unexpected source: Peter Galbraith. He had been a friend at Radcliffe and now worked for a U.S. senator. On a visit to Pakistan, Peter demanded to visit Benazir. Perhaps the authorities feared trouble with the United States, which supplied billions of dollars in aid. Whatever their reasons, the police awakened Benazir and her sister the night before Peter's planned visit and told them to pack. They were going to join their mother in Switzerland.

✳

Benazir's skin split and peeled, coming off her hands in sheets.

It was not yet dawn by the time Benazir and her sister arrived in Geneva. Although her ear was blocked and numb, Benazir took deep breaths of cold, mountain air and felt relief. After years behind walls, she was truly free. She could travel, be with her family, and say what she wanted to say.

Benazir's mother and brother Mir were now living in Geneva. Benazir might have stayed in Switzerland and rested from politics. But rest was not what she wanted. She wanted to have her infected ear treated in England. London was the center of political activity for the PPP members who had fled after the coup. Since political parties were banned in Pakistan, leadership for the PPP could reasonably come from outside the country. It was Benazir's hope to provide that leadership. She stayed with her Aunt Behjat in London until she found a place.

Benazir, around 1982.

(Opposite page)
During the early 1980s, Benazir spent much time in England organizing various elements of the PPP. Here, she talks with Margaret Thatcher in front of the prime minister's official residence.

London's Heathrow airport was jammed with Pakistani well-wishers and the press when she arrived. "Have you come into exile?" the reporters asked. It would have been accurate to say yes, because she knew she could do nothing locked up in jail or behind the walls of her family's house in Karachi. But her years of political struggle had taught her to think like the people she wanted to represent. If she said yes, they might lose heart in Pakistan.

"Exile?" said Benazir. "Why should I go into exile? I am in England for medical treatment. I was born in Pakistan and I'm going to die in Pakistan. . . . I will never leave my country." The message was clear: Benazir Bhutto would be back.

But first she had to attend to her health. Her ear operation caused pain for a couple of weeks, but she was cared for by her mother. Nusrat had flown from Geneva to be with her and had rented an apartment. For several weeks, Benazir had to lie flat. Sitting caused her pain and nausea. When she finally could sit up, she found that reading and writing caused the pain and dizziness to return. She lay there, listening to the birds in the trees outside that she couldn't see. Slowly she recovered, though she was now deaf in one ear.

*

For several weeks, Benazir had to lie flat. Sitting caused her pain and nausea.

She did have trouble with a more disturbing problem: fear. On first arriving in London, she had received dozens of visitors at her Aunt Behjat's home. One day, her aunt spotted a car full of Pakistani men parked across from her building. When Benazir went out somewhere, the car followed. Her aunt was indignant. "You don't have to put up with that in this country," she snorted. She had telephoned Scotland Yard. The car soon disappeared. Still, Benazir was anxious about being followed. She couldn't stop herself from looking over her shoulder when she walked. Worse, her years of isolation made her afraid of normal city situations. She couldn't get used to crowds and noise. She found herself taking cabs everywhere. At times, when she did have to be on the street, her heart pounded. She couldn't catch her breath.

Benazir did not want anyone to know that she was anxious, however. Her courage had been talked about for years. She was the woman who preferred to go to prison rather than be silent about Zia's policies. So she learned to hide her fears and to calm herself by taking deep breaths. And she learned not to show too much emotion in public.

Politician

Many people tried to convince Benazir to leave politics. But Benazir had no intention of leaving London for any length of time. She wanted to establish herself as a leader in the PPP's fight against the Zia military rule.

How to keep that leadership was the question. Forty thousand political prisoners were still in jail in Pakistan. And London was so far away. Benazir thought it might be useful to show the world how cruel Zia had been to those he arrested for political reasons. Perhaps Zia would feel enough pressure to release them.

There were strong reasons why such a campaign should begin in the United States. The United States Senate was to vote on a bill to send over 3 billion dollars in aid to Zia. But a U.S. law declares that no aid may be provided to any country that consistently tortures people, imprisons them without charges, or denies them the right to freedom.

Certainly the Zia regime violated human rights. Benazir Bhutto thought the U.S. Congress did not yet understand the terrible conditions in her country. And so, in the spring of 1984, she flew to America.

Lobbying on Capitol Hill

A young woman from Pakistan, holding no official title, would normally have little chance of even talking to the senators and representatives in Washington. Fortunately, Benazir's father had been well known. Also, people like her friend Peter Galbraith now had some influence in the halls of government. So Benazir went around to various offices and was politely received. The legislators were less concerned about human rights than about the possibility of Pakistan's developing a nuclear bomb. They were willing to hold back aid to prevent its development.

Benazir's trip seemed not to have any immediate effect on U.S. policy. Party members in Pakistan were being arrested and sentenced to death. Something had to be done to bring pressure on Zia not to execute those men.

Her apartment became an office. All hours of the day and night people were there putting out their magazine, *Amal,* which meant "Action." *Amal* tried to keep people up-to-date on what was happening in Pakistan. After the magazine was printed, copies were sold to make money to smuggle issues into the jails in Pakistan.

Chapter 6

Another Death

Benazir, around age 36.

On July 17, 1985, Benazir flew to Cannes, a resort village on the French Riviera. Her mother had organized a family reunion there. A two-bedroom apartment had been rented near the Mediterranean for the month of July. At the foot of the hills, which were covered with olive trees and vineyards, was the rocky seashore. White sailboats circled on the water.

Benazir was hoping for a relaxed family gathering. Their last get-together had been tense. Benazir and Mir tended to get into arguments over politics. They had strong disagreements about how to unseat Zia, for example. Mir and Shah's involvement in the terrorist group that had hijacked the Pakistani airliner was one source of friction. The hijacking was the reason Zia had given for arresting Benazir, her mother, and 6,000 other Pakistani political activists.

Shah felt that his life was in constant danger. He certainly had good reasons. He and Mir were once shot at, and he had nearly been poisoned by a servant in his wife's family. A dog that had tasted the food first had died. As a result, Shah had bought both himself and Benazir bullet-proof vests. He had taken out a permit to carry a gun. Shah and Mir carried small vials of poison with them wherever they went. The poison worked in seconds. If either of them was captured by Zia's men, they would kill themselves rather than betray any of their group under torture.

Shah and his mother picked up Benazir at the airport. He and his wife Rehana had recently moved to Cannes. They had rented an apartment in the hills above Cannes for themselves and their daughter Sassi. Benazir had sent a case of mangoes from their homeland, and they laughed and joked on the way home.

Early the next afternoon, the doorbell rang. Suddenly Sunny flung open the door. Something was seriously wrong with Shah, she cried.

Then Mir came back, his face drawn. "He's dead," Mir said. They drove to Shah's apartment. It was true. Shah was lying on the carpet in the living room.

✴
. . . They would kill themselves rather than betray any of their group under torture.

Benazir's brothers, Shah (left) and Mir (right) speak at a press conference in London.

As the family stood there stunned, Rehana came in from the bedroom. She was dressed in a white linen suit, not a hair out of place, not a tear in her eye.

"Poison," she said. "He took poison."

Exactly what happened to Shah no one knows. The French police kept Shah's body for weeks running tests. Nothing definite was ever found. An empty vial of poison was discovered in the kitchen garbage. But the poison Shah carried should have worked instantly. Instead it took hours for Shah to die. Where was Rehana while her husband was dying? She said she was asleep. Evidently the French police did not believe her. They arrested her, charging her with failing to assist a person in danger. Later, she was released and disappeared with Sassi to America.

Other questions remained unanswered. How did Rehana, with a trial to face in France, slip away so easily to the United States? And why didn't she go for help in the first place?

The decision to take Shah's body back to Larkana, to bury him near his father, was a serious political decision. Mir could not return, and Benazir's mother wouldn't.

The possibility that she would be arrested upon her return to Pakistan did not stop

Benazir. She wanted her brother to be properly buried. And she was angry. She was convinced that Shah's death, like her father's, was the responsibility of the dictator Zia. Defiantly, she returned to Karachi with the coffin.

For Muslims, the rituals of death are sacred and more important than daily routines of work. Many other Pakistanis also blamed Zia for the death of the youngest Bhutto. The funeral turned into an anti-government rally. Tens of thousands of black-robed mourners traveled to Larkana for the ceremony. The small airport was ringed with black figures, as was the road leading toward Larkana.

It was a magnificent farewell to a 27-year-old son of Sind. In the blistering 125-degree heat, mourners showered the ambulance with rose petals. They carried pictures of Benazir, her mother and father. One picture showed Shah next to Ali Bhutto and bore the phrase "the Martyr's Son Has Been Martyred." These people certainly did not believe what the government newspapers had claimed, that Shah had died of alcohol and drug abuse. Two thousand vehicles followed the motorcade, a procession 10 miles long.

Five days later, Benazir was arrested.

Benazir and her mother arrive in France to testify for an investigation into the death of Benazir's brother, Shah Nawaz.

Chapter 7

Taking Democracy Home

Still grieving the loss of her brother, Benazir roamed the now empty rooms where she, Mir, Sunny, and Shah spent their childhood. If Benazir ever doubted the wisdom of choosing a life in politics, it must have been at that time. Her baby brother was dead. She was alone. Hundreds of thousands of people might cheer her in the streets, but Benazir ate alone, went to bed alone, and greeted the day alone.

This period was the quiet before the storm. Soon, things began to happen very fast. After two months of house arrest, Benazir was freed to go to France for an inquiry into Shah's death. Then, on December 30, 1985, under great pressure from the United States, Zia lifted martial law. He was finally returning Pakistan to democracy, he said.

Benazir in 1986.

(Opposite page)
Loyal supporters shower Benazir with rose petals in Karachi, Pakistan's capital.

Benazir returned at once to London and called a meeting of the executive committee of the PPP. Leaders from Pakistan and abroad gathered around her dining room table to talk about the Party's future. Although martial law had been lifted, elections were not to be held for several years. No one knew if political parties like the PPP could now organize. They had been banned for nearly nine years. In the past, Benazir had returned to her homeland as an individual, not as a party leader. Even then she was arrested. Did she dare go now to pressure Zia for elections?

Yes, it was time. The Party leaders agreed. A number of them who still faced old arrest warrants decided to return, too. Together, around the table, they planned the cities they would tour. They would organize demonstrations all over Pakistan and demand that the regime call elections immediately.

To draw attention to their test of Zia's democracy, Benazir flew to Washington, D.C. There she met with legislators who had supported her before.

Then, back in London, she announced the date of her return to Pakistan. As hoped, the press flocked to London to cover the dramatic confrontation. The

more international attention she got,
Benazir reasoned, the less chance she had
of being arrested.

Finally the day came. The PPP had done
a good job. When her plane landed, the
airport was packed with a million people.
They had been there all night, and the
atmosphere was like a carnival. Food stalls
all along the road sold food and drink.
Formerly outlawed, the green, red, and
black banners of the PPP suddenly flut-
tered from every lamppost. Benazir
pushed through the crush of supporters
and climbed up on the platform of a truck
that would take them into the city. Friends
covered the truck with flowers.

It took 10 hours for the truck to travel
the few miles to the city. Benazir stood on
the platform for the entire time. Occasion-
ally, she rinsed her throat with some liquid
aspirin so as not to lose her voice.

"Do you want freedom? Do you want
democracy? Do you want revolution?" she
called out in Urdu, the national language.

"Yes!" the crowd roared back.

Scenes like this were repeated again and
again as Benazir and other PPP party leaders drove around the country. Benazir was
thrilled. Despite threats against her, she felt
safe surrounded by so many supporters.

To the Frontier

In an effort to reach people across Pakistan, Benazir took risks and traveled to dangerous places. In April, she paid a visit to a remote southwestern province. It is the poorest, most primitive part of the country. Ruled by tribal chiefs for years, no "outsider"—whether the British or Ali Bhutto—had ever been successful in changing it. Quarrels were solved with bullets. Benazir was entering a land where a Bhutto had few certain supporters.

The day she arrived, it was blazing hot. Benazir put ice cubes on her head and shoulders underneath her *dupatta* (scarf) to try to keep cool. As she sucked on lemons and salt, she prayed she wouldn't faint. Her guards circled tightly around her as they moved toward a revolving stage. Her security people had spotted three men squatting on their haunches at the front end of the crowd. Underneath their robes were automatic weapons. Three security guards were positioned directly in front of the men. If they moved suddenly, the guards would fall on them.

It turned out to be a peaceful rally. "It is not the law of God," cried Benazir, "that our people should live in poverty. The destiny of our nation is not slums. If we

❋

Quarrels were solved with bullets. Benazir was entering a land where a Bhutto had few certain supporters.

have the power to transform it through efficient use of our country's resources, then we must." The crowd rose and clapped. The danger had passed.

Violence was not to be avoided, however. Two weeks after this speech, the police ambushed and murdered Benazir's security chief. His companion was paralyzed by a bullet to the spine. Police also attacked demonstrators in Karachi on Pakistan Independence Day. This time, Benazir was with a classmate from Radcliffe, Anne Fadiman. Ann was writing an article for *Life* magazine. As the PPP caravan approached the site, clouds of teargas enveloped their jeeps. The police then tried to arrest them. The jeeps rushed back and forth across the city. Each time, they were blocked. Finally they were able to reach a public square. Smoke billowed from a burning bus as Benazir shouted through her public address system.

"You are all my brothers and sisters!" she cried. "Zia must go!" Abandoning the jeep, Benazir and Anne jumped into a car that stopped for them. But just as she was holding a press conference, three police-women arrived and took Benazir off to jail. She was ordered to spend 30 days in solitary confinement.

Chapter 8

Benazir Takes a Husband

Benazir did not stay in jail her full 30 days. Upon release, she returned to the house in Karachi. Martial law had been lifted, and she was free to go where she wished. Building the PPP and pressuring Zia for elections kept her busy in Pakistan.

The PPP still had a strong organization within Pakistan, with many loyal workers. The strength of the party was important, because Pakistan had a *parliamentary* system of government, similar to that of Great Britain. In a parliamentary system, the prime minister is not elected directly by the people, as in the United States. Instead, the prime minister is chosen by the political party that wins the elections. Benazir had been a leader in the party in London. Now she needed to prove to the other PPP leaders that the people would turn to her for leadership. If she led her party to victory in the elections, she would surely be appointed prime minister.

Benazir in 1989.

(Opposite page)
Benazir poses for a formal portrait with her husband and her first-born son.

But Pakistan had never had a woman in the national leadership. Benazir was asking her party to break with tradition. There were women in other Asian countries who had proved they could lead their countries. Indira Ghandi was prime minister of neighboring India. Corazon Aquino swept the Marcos dictatorship out of power in the Philippines. Both of these women, like Benazir, belonged to old, powerful, and political families. The popularity of their families' names had helped them to overcome a great deal of resistance because they were women.

And yet, in order to even consider being prime minister of Pakistan, Benazir needed to get married. She was very practical about it. In her autobiography she wrote that "in the male chauvinist society we live in . . . [there was] the bias that there must be something wrong with a woman who wasn't married." This was especially true in a Muslim society. So Benazir did the easiest thing: she had her mother arrange a marriage.

Benazir did not want people to think she was advocating arranged marriage. But it was the best solution for her as a Muslim woman, a popular leader, and an important career politician.

❋
. . . There must be something wrong with a woman who wasn't married.

There had been other opportunities for marriage in the past, of course. But Benazir had had many reasons not to consider them. Soon after she returned from the university, her father was imprisoned. Two years later, he was executed. After that, she was either in prison or locked up in her own house. When she did get away to England, she says that she was too shaky—too wound up—to think about getting married. But now, at the age of 34, it was finally time.

Auntie Manna, a sister of Benazir's father, was convinced her candidate was the most suitable. Asif Zadari was his name. He was just Benazir's age, and as handsome as any of the Bhutto men. His family, like the Bhuttos, owned land in Sind, and his father was vice-president of the Awami National Party, a political ally of the PPP. Asif had studied abroad and he played polo. He was the heir to the chiefdom in a province where Benazir most needed political allies.

Auntie Manna arranged a dinner party in Karachi, and without telling Benazir, invited Asif. At the time, Benazir did not know he was the chosen groom, but she remembers that as soon as they had been introduced they got into an argument.

Things got better later, in spite of the bad start. Before agreeing to anything, Benazir had a meeting with Asif's stepmother. Benazir presented Mrs. Zadari with every obstacle she foresaw.

Politics were the center of her life, Benazir warned. By this she meant that her her husband and family would not occupy that center, as was expected of Muslim women. Mrs. Zadari assured her that Asif understood. Benazir said that she would have to travel a lot, and that she couldn't always take her husband with her. This was crucial to Benazir, even though Pakistani women were usually not permitted to go places alone. In spite of custom, Benazir added, she could not live with her in-laws. Mrs. Zadari agreed; Asif's mother and sister would need privacy, too.

The only thing that remained was to spend time with Asif. It began with coffee at Auntie Manna's in London. The next day, he sent her a dozen roses, a crate of mangoes, and a box of French candy. Benazir claims that the roses didn't move her, but the sweets made a good impression. On July 29, 1987, her mother announced the engagement.

Their wedding was traditional and grand, political and personal, and it went on for

Benazir and Asif greet guests at their wedding reception in Karachi in 1987.

several weeks. School friends came to Karachi from the United States and England. Fifteen thousand invitations were sent to PPP supporters who had been imprisoned during martial law. Two hundred friends and family celebrated in a ceremony at the family house in Karachi. They ate and sang under colorful tents set up in the garden, and then drove in a procession to the public gathering. Over 200,000 loyal followers packed a local parade ground.

"Well," her friend Samiya joked afterwards, "now Zia won't call for elections until Benazir starts a family."

Chapter 9

Madame Prime Minister

Benazir addresses supporters outside her home in Karachi.

On August 17, 1988, Benazir was in a meeting with party workers when a journalist interrupted with an urgent call. A plane carrying General Zia had crashed after leaving a military base near the capital city. Many high-ranking officers and the U.S. ambassador to Pakistan were also on the plane. All aboard were killed, including General Zia. There was jubilation in the streets of Karachi, but Benazir was publicly cautious. Her public statements urged calm. She sent a letter of sympathy to the widow of the U.S. ambassador.

Acting President Khan called for elections on November 16, 1988, one day before Benazir's baby was expected. As Benazir's friend had predicted, their opponents hoped to prevent her from campaigning. Amazingly, the birth was premature, and Benazir's first child, a healthy, seven-pound son, was born in September.

Within five days, Benazir was being carried downstairs to her office and was putting in 18-hour days on the campaign.

Her work brought good results. On November 17, Benazir and the PPP won the elections. At the age of 35, just short of her first wedding anniversary, Benazir was sworn in as prime minister of democratic Pakistan. Immediately, she pardoned all political prisoners and restored full freedom of speech to the press.

The Hardest Part

As hard as she worked to become prime minister, her greatest challenge lay ahead. The problems she faced in making Pakistan a stable and prosperous modern nation were huge. The democratic institutions her father created—a constitution, independent judges, a parliamentary form of government, religious freedom and civil rights for all, including women—had been swept away by Zia's dictatorship. Seventy-seven percent of Pakistanis could not read or write. Bribery, crime, and smuggling were commonplace.

Weapons were cheap and easy to obtain. Armed bandits attacked travelers and villagers. They robbed, murdered, and held entire families for ransom.

Protesters conduct a "mock funeral" for Prime Minister Benazir Bhutto in front of the Pakistani embassy in New Delhi.

Under his policy of making Islamic law the law of the nation, Zia had given much power to the Muslim priests, or *mullahs*. One result was that religious minorities, who had had full civil rights under Ali Bhutto, were terrorized. Women, also, had suffered greatly from strict Muslim laws. Women who were raped were charged with adultery. They were sentenced to public lashings and prison unless they could provide male eyewitnesses to support their story.

Benazir spoke out against these injustices. But the greatest problem Benazir faced as Pakistan's leader was the desperate poverty of her people. Neither she nor the PPP were able to improve the standard of living in Pakistan. And this made it nearly impossible for real democracy to thrive.

Growing Problems

As Benazir's government continued to rule Pakistan, social problems and public unrest grew steadily out of control. More than 18 months after she took charge, most of her campaign promises remained unrealized. Benazir had promised to bring a new time of democracy and social change to Pakistan. Instead, gang violence, kidnappings, and murder were commonplace on the streets. Some of Pakistan's most dangerous areas were Sukkur and Larkana, native Bhutto country. "During the Zia years, the people used to fear the government," one Pakistani resident said at the time, "now the people fear the people."

The problems that spread throughout Pakistan greatly weakened Benazir's government. Charges of corruption and favoritism also dealt a blow to the prime minister. Finally, in August of 1990, Pakistan's President Ishaq Kahn dismissed Benazir's government. The president noted charges of corruption and poor leadership with his dismissal. Kahn called for new elections to be held in October and November.

The ousted prime minister casts her vote during popular elections in November of 1990.

The next blow came to Benazir on October 24, 1990. It was on that date that the Pakistani Parliament held its new elections. Benazir and her PPP were badly beaten. The opposition party, the Islamic Democratic Alliance, won in a great victory. Benazir charged that she lost due to "massive rigging" of the votes. And she vowed that her fight was not over. Provincial elections (popular elections where the citizens of the towns vote) were still to come. Benazir was sure the people of Pakistan would still support her.

✳
". . . The people used to fear the government, . . . now the people fear the people."

Nawaz Sharif replaced Benazir as prime minister of Pakistan after elections were held in 1990.

The results of the popular election shocked Benazir. Not only did she lose by a great margin, she hadn't even carried her hometown region. As the results came in, Benazir charged fraud. "I am angry and shocked at the way the elections have been rigged," she said. But the people of Pakistan had sent their message. And, after only 20 months in power, Benazir Bhutto's government would be no more.

Since she stepped down, Benazir has been faced with many other problems. Several misconduct and corruption cases against her could keep her out of politics for years to come. Criminal charges against her husband could send him to prison for decades. And the lack of support for her in her own country has made Benazir feel once again like an individual without a country.

The string of defeats Benazir faced in 1990 was, indeed, crushing. But she is no stranger to hard times. She has overcome hardships and losses much greater than those of politics. And each time, Benazir has surprised the world with her remarkable ability to improve her circumstances and come back. That is why many people still believe that Pakistan has not seen the last of Benazir Bhutto.

Glossary
Explaining New Words

burqa The black veils that many Muslim women wear when they leave their quarters or are in the presence of strangers.

coup A military seizure of power (pronounced "coo").

dupatta A scarf Muslims wear to cover their heads.

feminism A doctrine advocating equal rights for women.

Hindu A religious minority in Pakistan.

Islam The religion of the majority in Pakistan; a religion based upon the teachings of the prophet Muhammed; Muslims collectively.

Koran The collection of laws of Islam.

Mecca The birthplace of Muhammed and the most holy city of Islam, located in Saudi Arabia.

mullah A Muslim priest.

Muslim A believer in Islam.

muezzin The person that calls Muslims to prayer.

PPP Peoples Party of Pakistan, a political party founded by Ali Bhutto, and then led by Benazir Bhutto.

pilgrimage A journey to a sacred place.

purdah The Muslim practice of secluding women.

Sind A province in southern Pakistan that is the family home of the Bhuttos; Sindi is the language spoken in the Sind province.

shalwar khameez The national dress of Pakistan, consisting of baggy trousers and a long tunic.

Urdu The official language of Pakistan.

For Further Reading

Bhutto, Benazir. *Daughter of Destiny: An Autobiography.* New York: Simon and Schuster, 1989.

Desmond, Edward W. "The Undoing of Benazir." *Time,* 29 Jan. 1990: 56.

Galbraith, Peter W. "The Return of Benazir Bhutto." *Harvard Magazine,* July-Aug. 1989: 19–25.

Reeves, Richard. *Passage to Peshawar: Pakistan Between the Hindu Kush and the Arabian Sea.* New York: Simon and Schuster, 1989.

Richter, William L. "Pakistan under Benazir Bhutto." *Current History,* Dec. 1989: 435+.

Index

Photo credits:
Cover: © P. Smith/Gamma-Liaison; page 4: © Arvind Garg; pps. 5, 7, 8, 11, 13, 17, 20, 23, 29, 31, 43,
45, 55, 56: AP/World Wide Photos; p. 10: © Snowdon/Globe Photos; p. 14: © Roger Hutchings/
Globe Photos; pps. 18, 51: United Nations; p. 19: Camera Press/Globe Photos; p. 24: © Jim Bourg/
Reuters/Bettmann Newsphotos; pps. 26, 59: © Chip Hires/Gamma-Liaison; p. 27: © Richard Open/
Globe Photos; pps. 32, 35: © David Lomax/Camera Press/Globe Photos; p. 34: © De Keerle/Gamma-
Liaison; p. 40: © Kim Sayer/Globe Photos; p. 42: © P. Skingley/UPI/Bettmann; pps. 44, 60:
© Muzammil Pasha/Reuters/Bettmann; p. 50: Karsh of Ottawa/Camera Press/Globe Photos; p. 58:
© Kamal Kishore/Reuters/Bettmann.

Photo Research by Inge King.